108 Bridges Between Wellness & You !!

Evolve – Psychologically, Physically, Emotionally !!

Vishal Agarwal

ISBN: 9798672225913

"If you liked my book, hopefully you would want to know,
where it came from. Here I go…"

14 years ago, I started writing a book about 4 friends and a tri-nation trophy. As fate would have it, I never made it to the second page. Here I am, fortunately stuck in isolation, fulfilling my long lost dream. A dear friend once told me, "The four pillars that maketh a man are – plant a tree, raise a kid, build a start-up and write a book". I am thankful to lord for giving me the opportunity to construct my fourth pillar today.

I have spent the past decade trotting across the globe, selling diamond rings. Tired and exhausted, I sorely needed a long, long break off my business. I just wanted to stay at home, play with my son, sit with my family and live my hobbies. This lockdown could not have come at a more opportune time for me. I learned keyboard with my kid, read books and ticked a few points off my rusted bucket list. I even practiced yoga and Reiki and connected a bit with the spiritual world.

The year started for me by winning the National Jewellery Award for 'Best Diamond Ring of the Year'. It was followed by my lockdown story, and an amazing quarantine period, wherein I fell in love again with my own wife after a decade. The touch of courtship, of being close, yet so far; of being neighbours, yet connected only by video calls. It will be a memory to be cherished forever. Years later, when I look back, this is how I would want to recall the corona year of 2020. What is your story?

CONTENTS

Hello World!! It's a lovey planet and we just have one life to live. To add to it, there are a hundred ways to die and a thousand ways to live. THE CHOICE IS ALWAYS OURS. Let us begin with a simple act, close your eyes, take a deep breath, smile and think about your happiest moment of the day, month and year. Hey don't skip, this will take just a minute.

Are you smiling now? Back in the real world, it all feels so different. It is an all new world, with a "New Normal". However, the traditions of this new normal are all pre-historic, which our ancestors followed, from which we have moved on. Epidemics and pandemics are not new to mankind. The bacteria & viruses existed even before humans evolved. Still we have evolved to be the dominant species of the planet, as Charles Darwin mentioned in the "Survival of the fittest" theory. As a species we have survived over a million threats, so what is so special about this Novel Corona Virus, "Covid-19"? It does seem to have access to Darwin's theory, is evolving by the day, and confusing the doctors.

After all, we are humans, the most intelligent species in the universe. We have developed our own unique ways to survive. Every day, I read about various novel ways to beat the virus, some home grown, some with advanced medical research. It will be unjustified to term any such technique as under-researched or unproven. It's because the human body is so complex, and each and every body on this planet is matchless and behaves in its own distinctive way, based on the body and mind's habits and exposure to varied elements.

So, how do we Live Virus-Free? An ideal practice would be to first consult your doctor or physician. However, the doctors are already over-burdened, unable to answer all the queries, and it is our responsibility to take basic care of our health and hygiene. Herewith, I have collated 108 novel ways to Live Virus-Free. These include the best practices adopted by doctors, proven by medical research, local medicines by regional practitioners or some home remedies. The purpose is simply to let people get access to various methods that have helped people fight the virus anywhere across the globe. These have been practiced and proven for either prevention, or cure, or both.

There have and will be difference of opinion amongst experts as to what is and what isn't approved by the medical associations. It thus, comes with a word of caution, "SEEK CLINICAL ADVICE BEFORE PROCEEDING WITH ANY OF THE TECHNIQUES MENTIONED IN THIS BOOK". Any opinion mentioned in this book is completely personal, and comes with an intention to help my friends to live a healthy and joyful life. Any Bias, towards any region or religion is completely unintentional. I will re-iterate the caution again, different bodies may react differently to various methods. For example, an Indian, whose body is used to spicy vegetarian Indian street food and live in hot conditions, may not possess the same immune system as a non-vegetarian Canadian, used to living in sub-zero temperatures.

This book is an interesting compilation of healthy lifestyles. Read it, to enjoy the journey. If you are unwell, unlock a quick recipe to fitness in the closing note.

I. Win the battle in your mind

As we say, war is won not on the battlefield, but on paper and in mind. A battlefield exists to execute your plans to perfection. Today, we are at war with virus. The best way to win it is being prepared and ward it off, the moment it tries to enter our home or body.

1. Stay Happy

The old cliché, 'Stay Positive, Stay Happy' is so true. In the new normal, however, the people are horrified to hear the doctors say, 'Your report says, you are Positive'. Jokes apart, it's important to take primary care of your health and hygiene. More important is to believe that virus exists in this world, I too may come in contact with it, but my body is strong enough to defend it. Worry reduces the immunity, and a strong will power, coupled with joyful thoughts, enhances our immunity.

Social isolation may be the need of the hour, but we have a conscious decision to make – "We can't go outside due to fear of virus" or "I will celebrate some me-time and spend good time with family". Personally, I have never played so much with my kid, or laughed as much as I did during the past 4 months. The situation is the same, but the perception matters. For people like us, these times have been a revelation, for we got to live our long lost hobbies.

2. Read Books

We all know it's important to stay positive, but is it possible? Governments are issuing advisory on how to stay positive during isolation. We are bogged down by our home, work, business and family pressures. And to add to it, the fear of covid-19. I can say this with my personal face-off with the virus. It is scary.

We all know that virus has hit our town, but somewhere we believe, we are taking our necessary precautions and thus, we are safe. The day, we or our family member gets our first symptoms, we start feeling the heat. In spite of our utmost precautions, there are very high chances that virus will spread to a few more family members. The recovery rate of the virus is excellent, but it is psychologically very draining. It is normal to worry about your family, parents and kids. But more important to believe, that it will soon pass away.

One of the best guide and motivators are books. It keeps us busy, engrossed and helps us prevent wild thoughts. There are not many things that one can do in isolation. Thus, most of our time is spent on mobiles, tablets or TV. Books also helps us reduce our screen time. My first couple of days with fever were filled with worrying thoughts about my family. It heavily dented my recovery. Third day, I got some self–help books for myself, including Robin Sharma and Sadhguru; Some magazines and religious books for my parents; story books for kids, including Hardy Boys and Famous Five. Our recovery rate improved immediately. In 2-3 days, we felt much healthier.

3. Talk to Cheerful Friends

We are selective with what we eat, and prefer to eat healthier. It's OK to eat some chocolates and sweets once in while in small portions. It keeps us refreshed. Are we equally choosy in feeding our brain with positive thoughts? We keep watching news of crime and impending economic gloom and receive more on social media.

Instead, talk to your friends and family cheerfully, about the great things you did during lockdown, things for which you could never find time. There's just one way to come out of crisis, "Look at it as an opportunity, and capitalise on it". Here's one approach to evade negativity, "Talk to positive people". Feed your mind with the positive conversations about your business, education, travel escapades and future plans.

II. Breathing Exercises

Once you are strong mentally, you need to develop physical immunity to ward away the virus. A healthy diet and workout are among the most common ways to develop immunity. My foremost recommendation is the breathing exercises from the Vedas, popularized recently by yoga gurus like Baba Ramdev and Sri Sri Ravi Shankar amongst others. The hand-picked exercises mentioned below are the ones, which increases the oxygen intake and processing capacity of lungs and heart respectively. These are the first organs attacked by covid-19. If the oxygen supply in the blood are maintained, the body's ability to fight the virus improves dramatically.

Ideal time to perform it is between 5 am to 7 am in the morning. One may also repeat it in the evening. It should be performed at least 2 hours after a meal, or minimum 15 minutes before a meal.

For first timers, it is recommended to learn the techniques under a trained yoga practitioner. Optionally, you may refer to YouTube videos of Baba Ramdev or Sri Sri Ravi Shankar.

4. Bhastrikā

Bhastrikā is the first of the 3 to 5 breathing exercises recommended by yoga gurus. It involves deep inhalation and forceful exhalation of breath. It drains excess phlegm from the lungs, oxygenates the blood, and increases the vitality of organs and tissues. Do it for 4-5 minutes followed by Kapāl-bhāti. Force and duration may vary as per one's capability. Heart patients should do it less forcefully.

Bhastrikā pranayama also cleans our nasal passage and kills any germs or virus in the initial stages.

5. Kapāl-Bhāti

Kapāl-bhāti is formed from two words, kapāl meaning 'skull', and bhāti meaning 'shining'. The kapāl-bhāti exercise is a sequence of forceful exhalations, and inhalation happens automatically. It helps in cleaning of the sinuses, and is considered to be the most important and effective of all the breathing exercises. Kapāl-bhāti not only strengthens the lungs, but also removes blockages in heart. It is also recommended by many physicians, though there haven't been any clinically authored tests to its name.

Kapāl-bhāti is one such exercise, one must try and learn in these circumstances. There have been instances of people suffering from cardiac arrest during work-outs. A cardiac arrest while performing a breathing exercise is unheard of, in a country where millions practice Kapāl-bhāti daily. It is the most common breathing exercise suggested by doctors and physicians.

6. Anulom-Vilom

Anulom - vilom is a technique of breathing alternatively with our two nostrils. It's a simple procedure, inhale from the first nostril, exhale from the second, then inhale from the second nostril and exhale from the first. Our right nostril is associated with Sun, or body's heating energy, and left nostril is associated with Moon, or body's cooling energy. This pranayama, balances the warm and cold energy in our body and helps cure physical and mental ailments.

This exercise not only enhances the functioning of lungs, but also helps fight nervousness and reduce stress level. It is specially recommended to patients suffering from anxiety or depression.

7. Sudarshan Kriya

It is a special breathing technique, designed by yoga guru Sri Sri Ravi Shankar. It is series of systematic inhalation and exhalation with 3 stages of speed. This technique is taught by thousands of trained teachers who are part of the NGO 'Art of Living'.

Sudarshan Kriya is also claimed to have worked wonders for hundreds of physical ailments, including depression, hypertension, diabetes, asthma, digestive and respiratory illness. It is advised to perform this breathing exercise only after learning under trained teacher and not just from videos.

8. Jal-naiti

Jal-Naiti or anterior nasal wash, is a simple ancient yogic procedure to cleanse any virus which may have entered our nostrils. Majority of the covid-19 virus enters our body via our nostrils and it takes them a couple of hours or days to spread inside. Doctors (treating covid-19 patients) at Deenanath Mangeshkar hospital at Pune have kept themselves safe from getting infected by performing this simple procedure twice a day.

First, do ten rounds of kapāl-bhāti with each nostril (other nostril closed), then ten rounds with both the nostrils open, to clean the nasal passage. Then take lukewarm water in a small pot with a dispenser. Bend your head forward, tilt it on one side and slowly pour water from one nostril, such that it comes out from another. Then repeat it with another nostril. Caution: The water should not go inside your nasopharynx or wind-pipe; breathe from your mouth while performing it; and learn from a trained person, before performing Jal-naiti.

III. Physical work-out

A 30 minutes work-out is essential for physical and mental fitness. It assists in prevention as well as in treatment of covid-19. A recent government survey said, blood samples of 21,387 random people were tested in Delhi. 23.48% of these people had covid-19 antibodies.

People who are physically and mentally fit, have better immunity. They have a lower chance of getting any symptoms, even if they have contracted the virus.

Work-out is also important in recovering from illness. Most fever including covid-19 renders a patient weaker, even after recovery. Work-out is even suggested in mild forms, as body permits, for patients, for faster recovery. Patients should not over stretch themselves, as heart and lungs are already weaker, and oxygen saturation levels may not be very high.

9. Brisk Walking

Brisk walking is the best exercise advised by most medical practitioners across the globe. Ideal pace for brisk walking is 5-6 km/hr. A 20-60 mins walk per day is the most optimum solution to keep all diseases at bay.

a) Brisk-walking strengthens heart and lungs.
b) Walk barefoot on the grass, it improves blood circulation and improves eye-sight.
c) Regular walking strengthens our leg muscles.
d) Brisk walking checks hypertension, blood sugar and cholesterol levels.
e) Post dinner 20 mins walk helps keep our digestive system fit.
f) Morning walk during sunrise builds immunity. Just breathe in fresh air and get maximum vitamin D from sunlight.

10. Running

Running or jogging is one of the best ways to stay fit. It strengthens our heart, lungs and muscles and maintains our body vitals, including blood pressure, cholesterol, hormonal balance, pulse, sugar levels, burns calories and extra fat. A good work-out is also a perfect dose for a happy brain.

Primary tips for running: Choose the right footwear for running; learn ideal body posture, to prevent harm to your ankles and knees; adequately re-hydrate yourself; basic warm-up exercise before running and stretching exercises after running.

11. Cycling

Cycling is the third most popular cardio exercise globally practiced. It has almost all the benefits of running or jogging. It increases cardiovascular fitness, reduces obesity, improves health of heart and lungs, builds muscles and reduces stress level. A cycling enthusiast never ceases to cycle. It is not just for the physical fitness that comes along, but more importantly the mental fitness and freshness you feel after cycling.

For best results, ensure the basic techniques are practiced, including, ideal cycle size, seat height, handle position, your body posture while cycling, optimum tyre pressure and proper foot-wear. These are to ensure that you do not injure yourself while cycling. Improper body posture can cause back-ache or stress on lower back bone, improper seating position may stress your knees. Regular cycling enthusiasts should ensure that the seat and handle positions are customised for your height by a professional.

12. Cardio Exercises

The importance of cardio exercises has increased in current times. One of the best chances to fight the covid-19 virus is by having a strong pair of lungs and heart. Cardiovascular exercise ensures a healthy heart and reduces stress levels. A few of the cardio exercises require particular equipments; if you have any of them, it's great, else there are a number of exercises you can do at home without specific equipments. Here's a list of a few common cardio exercises. You may contact your gym instructor for ideal work-out schedule as per your body's requirements.

a) Treadmill
b) Swimming
c) Rowing
d) Step-up, Step down
e) Burpees

f) Climbing stairs

g) Jogging at same place

h) Jumping

i) Skipping

13. Dance or Aerobics

Dance and Aerobics have an added advantage over other cardio exercises, it is also an expression of art. It thus, is a perfect stress buster. While walking, running or cycling are outdoor exercises, dancing has gained one of the top spots of indoor exercises during isolation. Music relaxes the mind and mood, while work-out refreshes the body. Excessive sweating while dancing also reduces chances of a fever. So, like in other cardio exercises, allow your body to naturally cool down after the dance work-out. Prefer warm water or room-temperature water immediately after work-out.

14. Warm up and Stretching

Warm up before any exercise, work-out or dance is essential to shake the body from resting to active state. It prevents injury to muscles, as all the muscles gradually warms up and gets prepared for a work-out. Similarly, post work-out stretching is required to cool down the body. For a list of warm up exercises and stretching exercises, you may consult your gym instructor or check online. I will though stress more on what is important for covid-19 patients.

The recovery plus isolation period of a patient ranges from 14 to 28 days. Most of the time is spent resting on bed with mild to severe weakness. A common observance is a sore body, with stiff back and rusted joints. It is thereby, advisable for all such patients to do a little warm up, joint rotation and body stretching exercises daily. Do not tire yourself out, if you are a patient, and take a deep breath after every exercise. If weakness is more, then perform only the ones, which can be done lying on the bed, without consuming much energy.

15. Surya-Namaskār

Surya namaskār is one of the oldest exercise known to mankind. It has been refined and handed down over generations since Vedic era. Surya namaskār literally means Saluting the Sun. It is a series of 12 postures or āsanas in a particular sequence. It is suggested to be performed in front of rising sun for maximum benefits.

Surya-namaskār encapsulates the best of all yoga āsanas. It alone completes the body's work-out requirement. It reduces obesity, tones our body muscles, stretches all body parts, builds stamina, improves body flexibility, improves digestive system, controls cholesterol and blood sugar levels and helps fight anxiety. It thus, is a complete immunity as well as strength builder.

16. Bathe in the Morning Sun

Vitamins are very vital to keep you alive, and you don't always have to pay for it. Give yourself ample of sunlight daily. Vitamin D is thereby also known as 'Sunshine Vitamin'. Are you worried about getting tanned? Yes, you should be. So don't stay in the sun for too long. 15-30 minutes of morning sun just after sunrise is sufficient for most people. You may enjoy this time playing or walking in a garden; praying to sun-god; do Surya namaskār, the yogic exercise; or simply enjoy your morning tea, bathing in the sun.

IV. Eat Healthy

Healthy eating habits are always a concern of parents for their children. However, they never develop the ideal eating habits, and rightly so. A child never learns what their parents teach them, they simply follow what their parents do. So, if you want your kids to eat healthy, then you will have to govern your taste buds.

In covid-19 times, when people are scared, your only option is to eat what your body requires. All these pills of calcium, vitamins and proteins are currently widely in demand, as people are suddenly conscious of building a healthy body. Rightly so, these are necessary in the short term to stay fit. However, our body has been designed to stay fit, if we eat right and work-out regularly. All the nutrients that our body require, works best, if we consume them in their natural form, i.e. eat healthy.

17. Vitamin C

Vitamin C is one of the most easily available nutrient in the food we eat. Lemon water is a refreshing source of Vitamin C and tastes great in warm water as well as with ice. Orange, amla, sweet lemon, lime and other citrus fruits, berries, kiwifruit and blackcurrants are some common fruits rich in Vitamin C. Vegetables like red and green pepper, broccoli, capsicum, cauliflower, spinach, cabbage, and other leafy vegetables, tomatoes and sweet potatoes give a wide option of food rich in Vitamin C. It is again richer if we consume them raw, as uncooked salad or as boiled vegetable soup.

18. Vitamin D

Vitamin D helps in absorption of calcium in the gut. It is therefore, necessary for bone growth. Vitamin D1, 2 and 3 are the ones which are not richly found in fruits and vegetables. For a vegan, the richest source of Vitamin D is sunlight. Vegetarian options are cereals, orange juice, milk, milk-products such as cheese, cottage cheese, tofu etc. Mushrooms, egg yolks, fatty fishes like salmon, tuna and mackerel and herring are other sources of Vitamin D.

19. Vitamin B

There are 8 vitamins under Vitamin B, collectively known as B-complex. Though each of these have their distinctive functionality, collectively they help our body to produce energy and in development of certain molecules.

Vitamin B again is richly available in animal products like fish, meat, eggs and poultry. Vegetarian options similarly are milk, milk products and cereals. Yeast and mushrooms are other options consumed by some vegetarians also. Seasonal fruits and vegetables like beetroot, sprouted Alfalfa, apple, mango, orange, potato and butternut squash also contain Vitamin B in smaller quantities. Vitamin B9 is richly available in leafy vegetables like spinach, lettuce, cabbage, turnip etc. Vitamin B12 deficiency is a cause of concern for vegetarians. However, low to regular requirements for B12 is met by regular intake of cereals and wholegrains like barley.

20. Other Important Nutrients

Apart from the above, a body generally needs Vitamin E, Vitamin A, Folic Acid, Iron, Zinc and Selenium to develop a strong immune system. There is no better way of nutrient intake than eating raw seasonal fruits and vegetables. Supplements are not necessary to meet your body's daily requirements. It is only advised because of unhealthy eating habits.

21. Drink Warm Water

Regular intake of warm water kills the virus in the early stages, if it has spread till mouth and throat. So it is a precaution as well as the first line of defence against the virus. Apart from the virus, warm water twice a day keeps our digestive system healthy. If someone has diabetes, check his blood sugar level, drink warm water first thing in the morning, for 7 consecutive days and check the blood sugar again. There will be a sharp improvement. A glass of warm water just before going to bed, reduces chances of a cardiac arrest. It helps in weight loss and lower LDL cholesterol.

22. Soup and Fresh Juice

Include soups and fresh juices to your daily diet. Hot vegetable soup is great for patients. In case of throat pain, or indigestion, soup serves as a great option, as they are easy to digest and retains the necessary fibres. Choose the veggies as per taste and availability.

Fresh juice without any added sugar should be our ideal replacement for all the carbonated drinks. They are healthy and nutritious. For sweet lovers suffering with diabetes, fresh juice serves as the perfect alternative. As per nutritionists, most juices are harmful for a diabetic patient because of the added sugar and preservatives. Fresh juices instead, without extra sugar and without filtering the fibres are great for health, as natural sugar is easily processed by the body.

23. Kādhā

Kādhā or a herbal potion is very effective in boosting our immunity. These can be easily made at home with commonly available ingredients. It is also an effective medicine to fight seasonal flu, infections and common cold. Ingredients include moti elaichi (cardamom), kachi haldi (fresh turmeric), laung (cloves), kali mirch (black pepper), tulsi (holy basil leaves), dal chini (cinnamon), adrak (ginger), munakkā (raisin) and honey (as per taste). A simple way to make is, boil some water, peel and crush all the ingredients and add to the boiling water. Let it boil for 15-20 minutes, filter it and drink it like a tea before going to bed. Ready-made kādhā powder is also supplied by many ayurvedic pharma shops, NGO's and social groups supplying from home.

24. Tulsi

Tulsi or holy basil leaf is among the best antibiotics as mentioned in the Vedas. Regular intake of 5 Tulsi leaves every morning is a great immunity booster. Alternatively, put a few leaves in a jar full of water and drink it throughout the day. It helps to detox our body. Having a pot of Tulsi plant inside your home also has its advantages. A Tulsi plant is among the few plants which releases oxygen (and little ozone) 24 hours a day.

It is considered to be a sacred plant and prayed as a goddess since Vedic ages. Any food serving, which we offer to our lords, is incomplete without

Tulsi leaves. There is an old Hindu tradition of keeping a Tulsi plant in the porch of a house, and watering it first thing in the morning. The underlying purpose of marking it sacred is to make sure that it is followed religiously as a tradition for generations. Eat the leaves fresh, first thing in the morning for a healthy life. The bark of Tulsi plant is also used in many medicines.

25. Neem

A couple of fresh neem leaves intake in the morning purifies the blood. It also aids in de-clotting of the blood vessels, and is good for patients having diabetes or hypertension. It has been used since ancient times to cure multiple diseases of stomach, heart, liver and ailments such as fever or infections. Neem leaves are also burned to cleanse air inside a house, as its smoke kills airborne bacteria.

26. Chyawanprash

Chyawanprash is a traditional Indian food supplement. Its history is as old as the Indian culture with earliest recorded ayurvedic recipes found in *Charak Samhita*. There are numerous formulations of it and most ayurvedic pharma companies have their own variation of a chyawanprash. It is a concoction of more than 50 herbs with amla being the prime ingredient. It is a complete supplement with necessary nutrients and minerals.

One teaspoon per day is sufficient for our daily requirements. It can be taken throughout the year, and is especially recommended during onset of winters. Herewith, I have mentioned a number of healthy food options. Chyawanprash, is one such thing which encompasses the benefits of most herbs. It is a strong immunity builder, revitalises our body, purifies blood, fulfils any nutrient deficiency, improves digestive system, improves body endurance, and balances all the body functions. Its necessity has increased more so because of its ability to protect and strengthen our respiratory system, which is most susceptible today to the virus.

27. Patanjali Immunity Boosters

Ayurvedic or herbal medicines have one very positive aspect, i.e. nil or minimal side effects. Ayurvedic medicines are made directly from herbs, with low amount of added chemicals. These are almost as good as eating healthy food, rather than taking supplements.

Patanjali has come up with a few immunity boosters, which improve our body vitals, provide requisite amount of nutrients and thus help build immunity.

1) Arogya Vati: it is an anti-viral, an antibiotic and an immunity booster as well. It is advised for shielding as well as to help fight the virus.
2) Giloy Ghanvati: It helps our body fight fever, common cold and is effective even for patients with hypertension, diabetes, cancer and other ailments.
3) Tulsi Ghanvati: It again is a medicinal version of Tulsi leaves and has same benefits as eating Tulsi leaves.

28. Avoid Junk Food

Eat healthy, that is the bare minimum we can do to give our body as much strength and nutrients to fight the virus. Colas, chips, chocolates, ice-creams and spicy street food may keep our spirits high, but it consumes a lot of energy of our body to process them. More so, they do not contribute much to the nutrient requirements of our body. Instead of building muscles and bones, it adds to the lazy fat and cholesterol contents of body.

Occasionally, we all crave to spoil ourselves. Go ahead and enjoy your favourite delicacy, but do prefer home cooked meal as much as possible. The recent lockdown period has created lots of chefs, who have uploaded online, tons of recipes of super healthy and delicious salads, and most delicacies you can think of.

29. Avoid Uncooked Animal Food

Recently the world has seen a steep increase in virus contracted from animals. Right from Swine flu, covid-19, plague, H1N1 and HIV have all created havoc in human lives. It is thus strongly suggested to avoid uncooked animal food. It is also noteworthy, to keep high sanitisation in place while cooking animal food, as the chances of virus spreading are high even while preparing the food. In several cases, it has been advised to even avoid raw eggs. Well cooked food, almost destroys any virus present.

30. For Hostellers and Paying Guests

Eat healthy food at home is the most common advice we all can get and give. However, for millions of students and working people, who stay alone away from home, this may not be even an option. The only options are dining out, take away, home delivery, tiffin or packed food. Having said that, eating healthy cannot be negated. Choose what you order or eat. Avoid packed food.

Increase an intake of fresh fruits and order healthy salads. You can also prepare salads at your hostels and flats easily with handpicked vegetables and mouth-watering dressings. In case you dine out or order restaurant food, choose to eat hot and freshly cooked food.

31. Reduce Smoking and Tobacco

Yes, you heard it right. Reduce the tobacco intake and the number of cigarettes one smokes per day. Do not stop it all at once today. Our body gets heavily addicted to tobacco or respective drugs that one may smoke. Quitting will require medical support and therapies, which is tough to find today, in the prevalent situation.

So what is the need to even reduce it today? It's because these drugs take a heavy toll on our immunity and smoking badly damages our lungs. Weak lungs cannot fight the mildest variations of corona virus, and the infections spread very fast. The oxygen processing capacity of the lungs of a smoker is low, which means he may require oxygen support more than others. Its simple maths, keep your lungs alive, and your lungs will keep you alive.

V. Preventive Social Care

It is important to believe that the novel corona virus is not a deadly virus, it is just very, very contagious. If it touches you, no need to worry, you will recover within couple of days. You only have to make sure that you are absolutely isolated and do not spread the virus to your friends and family.

32. Maintain Social Distance

Every one of us would have heard this a thousand times in recent times, but do we follow it? After all, Man is a social animal. Without socialising, a man will go into depression. Online chats and meets doesn't give the feeling. Agreed. But, we surely can take the necessary precautions. Business meetings can be done online or across a long table wearing masks. Meet occasionally with family and friends to keep yourself fresh. Maintain a social distance, hugs and kisses can be restricted to only your family members (and perhaps one boyfriend / girlfriend).

33. Namaste or Ojigi

The new old way of greeting. Our ancestral culture may not have the swag, but is definitely wiser. The Indian way of greeting, Namaste is now the most respected way of greeting, taking a toll on handshakes. It not only protects us from spreading a virus, but is also a mark of giving regards. The Japanese Ojigi, or a gentle bow is also a polite greeting gesture, and is gaining popularity. Please don't worry about a sore back.

34. Wear Face Mask or Face Shield

Wearing a face mask and covering our nose and mouth is the foremost thing we need to do to prevent ourselves from inhaling any airborne virus. For doctors treating covid-19 patients, surgical masks or specifically designed N-95 masks are necessary. However, even as a day-to-day precaution, we should wear simple masks, made of cloth, tissue or non-woven material. Another option is a see-through face-shield, made of fibre or plastic.

35. Wear Gloves

When we are in a society or area where there are patients infected with covid-19, it is advisable to wear gloves in public places. It is also important to dispose the gloves in a sanitized way so that it doesn't infect others. If we are using re-usable gloves, it is necessary to wash them with a disinfectant after every use. While it is important to use masks and gloves, it is also noteworthy that we use environment friendly products, which are bio-degradable.

36. Use Hand-Sanitizer

While gloves cover your hands from getting in contact with the virus, a hand sanitizer does a better job, it kills them straightaway. A pocket sanitizer is now almost a mandatory carry-on. It though comes with a word of caution; it can be inflammable. Sanitizers are broadly available in 2 categories – gel based and alcohol based.

If you are using an alcohol based sanitizer, do not spray it near flames, electrical points or car ignition. Alcohol based sanitizers are also known to cause dryness or minor irritation. Avoid spraying near eyes or open wounds. These sanitizers are toxic in nature and should not be ingested or allowed any contact with food.

37. Wash Hands and Face

Places where water isn't available or hand-wash is not an option, hand-sanitizer is the ideal option. It's like, a hand sanitizer kills the virus, but their dead bodies are still stuck on your hands. Effectively, it means, virus is nullified but dirt isn't cleaned with a sanitizer. A very important preventive measure is hand wash and face wash whenever we reach office or come back home. Though most hand wash or face wash gels or soaps are reliable these days, a more preferable option would be to use anti-bacterial wash gels.

It is also advisable to change your clothes, first thing when you are back from work, in the evening. Only after that, touch anything at your home. Add a little antiseptic or disinfectant liquid to wash your clothes.

38. Wash Your Food or Cans

There are a hundred ways through which a virus can enter your home or body. No one can make it full-proof. But one can definitely put a check on persons or things that have entered our home. We sanitise ourselves and our clothes when we get back home. What about the food or grocery or shopping we did?

No need to panic, as the chances are glim that a virus may survive on multiple surfaces. However, at least till the level possible, we should take care to sanitise our shopping. As for food and vegetables, just put it under running tap water. One may also use warm water or salt water to clean fruits, vegetables or food packets. Never use soap water or sanitizer on fresh eatables.

39. Sanitise Your Home

People around us are getting infected and the virus is spreading like wildfire. Hygiene requirements are at its peak for us to survive. We not only need to sanitise and wash ourselves, but also the things we use, our home, society and work-places. It is vital to use sanitiser spray or wipe high contact surfaces like handles, doorknobs, switchboards, lift buttons of your office or home, table-tops of your home at least once a week. Caution: keep away from flames and electric sockets.

Sodium hypochlorite solution (10 ml in 10 lit water) can be used as spray to sanitise your society or your work-place. Phenol or other disinfectant can also be used be used to mop the flooring in your house. 1% sodium hypochlorite solution can be easily made at home using sodium hypochlorite bleach (containing 3.5% chlorine) or bleaching powder (70% chlorine).

40. Avoid Crowded Places

Luxury shopping gives us immense joy, a feeling we have been missing desperately. Perhaps for our own good. Shopping for necessities can't be avoided. But they surely can be reworked. Choose the shops, which are less frequented; pick a time say post lunch, when the crowd is at minimum and finish your shopping by visiting as minimum shops as required. So, you don't get to be choosy, pick the best dress, or cheapest grocery, but, you do increase your chances of staying alive, and consume what you have shopped.

41. Avoid Centralised Air Conditioner

Centralised air conditioners re-circulate the air that was present in a room. In a large mall or office space, if a covid-19 patient sneezes, the virus instantly gets airborne and is likely to get recirculated inside the vents of centralised air conditioners. This cool air, consequently aids the virus in scattering around and infecting more people.

42. WFH

Work from Home, the youngest acronym to hit the town comes with a lot of comfort zones. Flexi timings, cut down travel time, no pollution, and you can wear shorts with your formal jacket, without getting noticed. Flipside, you don't get a chance to impress your client or boss with your impressive personality and perhaps lose a deal. Many businesses are just not meant to flourish online. So, it will require a lot of hard work to survive. And the lazybones will have to do some real smart work and innovate to get lucky. While WFH is the need of the hour for safety reasons, it is also the time to be innovative in your work culture.

43. Check Your Symptoms

The common symptoms of covid-19 are fever, dry cough, shortness of breath, diarrhoea and loss of appetite. Other symptoms are sore throat, tiredness, body ache, loss of smell and taste. The symptoms may not be the same for everyone. However, high fever has been one of the most common symptoms with temperatures ranging from 102° F to 104° F for 3-5 days. There have been numerous asymptomatic cases as well. It is highly imperative to quarantine yourself, and inform people you may have come in contact with, as soon as you identify any symptoms.

VI. Stage one of defence

This is a very important moment, as soon as you have identified any symptoms of contracting the virus. 80% of the people who have contracted the disease are either asymptomatic, or do not require hospitalisation and medication. Using proper preventive measures doesn't only ensure faster recovery, but also ensures that it doesn't get transmitted to your friends and family.

44. Self-Isolation

Self-isolation or self-quarantine is mandatory to break the chain of virus transmission. The virus gets easily airborne from an infected patient via saliva droplets, as and when a person speaks, sneezes or even yawns. It then attaches itself to anything that the person wears, uses or touches. Corona virus can stay alive airborne, or on clothes, artefacts or food from a few hours to a few days. Governments across the globe has thus made it mandatory for people, to stay quarantined from 7 -14 days, who may have come in contact with the virus.

45. Get a Covid-19 Test

Once you have isolated yourself, it's imperative to get a covid-19 test at your nearest test centre. It helps you in taking respective care as per the test results. If the test results are positive, then extreme care is required to cure yourself and also prevent it from spreading. It is worth noting that it is great to know if the results are negative, but you cannot let the guard down for the next few days. It could be possible that your body may have fought off the virus, but you could still be a carrier of the virus. Though, as per World Health Organisation, the chances of it are minimal.

46. Steam

There has been no official confirmation from any research if steam kills the virus. Still, steam inhalation has been widely advised by doctors in many countries, not just as a preventive measure, but also as a cure in treating covid-19 patients. Steam inhalation for 2-3 minutes twice or thrice a day is said to kill the virus not just in the nasal passage and throat, but also the ones that have spread till the lungs. There have been numerous viral videos of covid-19 patients especially from Wuhan, the original epicentre of corona-virus claiming the only medicine they took to cure themselves is inhaling steam for a couple of minutes 4 times a day.

47. Gargle

Gargle with lukewarm salt water. It helps to cleanse your throat or cure sore throat. It is thereby, a preventive measure to keep corona virus at bay. Gargling with saline water has been widely prescribed by many ayurvedic doctors as one of the best preventive measures. It may be noted that gargle is not a cure. Also worth noting is that these preventive measures are regionally advised, however, globally, none of the measures have been full-proof in prevention against covid-19.

In case of sore throat, add a pinch of haldi (turmeric powder) in hot water. Repeat it twice a day. If you have a cough or phlegm, then boil some tea leaves and a pinch of salt in a glass of water. Filter and gargle with the water, as hot as you can comfortably use.

48. Drink Fluids

Drink a lot of water and fruit juices if you have fever symptoms. This helps our body on two fronts; there are chances of diarrhoea when you contract the SARS-CoV-2 virus, so fluid intake protects from dehydration; second, fresh fruits and juices are the rich sources of vitamins, fibres and glucose. These not only helps us fight the virus, but also ensures that our body doesn't feel weakness in the process.

Fluid intake can be in form of fresh juices, soups, coconut water, ORS solutions, barley water, milk or milk shakes, lemon water, glucose water, kādhā, or even juicy fruits. It helps to detox our body, flush out the virus, provides the vital nutrients and re-energises our body.

49. Bathe Twice a Day with Hot Water

The foremost priority is to prevent infections. One who is infected, may carry the virus all over his body, while eating, talking or during work-out. One of the best ways of checking the spread is by taking a bath with hot water twice a day. This kills most virus attached on your body, and will help you save your friends and family from getting infected.

50. Rest

As much as a work-out is required for a healthy body, so is rest required for the mind and body to relax and recharge. Give your body 6-8 hours of sound sleep, and more if you feel any weakness. Another rest that is important is that of our mind. For a body to recover, it is important to focus on the positive and healing energy. So, work from home during isolation is only advisable until it keeps you busy and not worried.

There is also a resting āsana, or meditative rest, known as *shavāsana* or corpse pose. This yogic rest is also practiced after yoga exercises to give the requisite amount of rest to our body post work-out. In case of a hectic schedule, when you cannot complete your sleep, a 20 minute *shavāsana* refreshes our body, similar to what a deep sleep does. This is also suggested to patients suffering from insomnia.

An advanced form of *shavāsana* is one where you lie down on your bed, in a silent room. Then, focus one by one on each body part for a minute each, starting from toes to head. Then imagine your body floating in space. Gradually, come back to your room and open your eyes.

VII. Ayurvedic and Home Remedies

Ayurvedic and home remedies has helped cure diseases for which the giant pharmaceutical companies do not have any answer. The ingredients, recipes and treatment methodology has been passed on from generations since the times of sages. Many of such treatments involve usage of commonly available herbs, which have penetrated millions of households. The flipside is that people know the right herbs, but not the right dosage. This either renders it ineffective or may lead to some side-effects also.

So, whenever you take any medicine or treatment, always use an expert advice of an experienced person. Blindly following a book or an advice on internet can be dangerous.

51. Amla

Amla is a good immunity booster. It is a rich source of Vitamin C. The first health supplement that a doctor will suggest a patient suffering with any viral fever is Vitamin C. One fruit of Amla has 600 mg to 700 mg of Vitamin C, which is sufficient to meet our daily requirement. A standard Vitamin C supplement commonly prescribed has 500 mg of Vitamin C. Our body has a natural tendency to absorb Vitamins from a natural juice more effortlessly than from a supplement.

Amla can be eaten fresh, or dried and eaten for days. Amla or Indian gooseberry, is a seasonal fruit, and freshly available in winters. It is suggestable to have 1 fresh Amla or its juice daily before breakfast. It purifies our body from the toxins. To enhance its taste, you can also add a little lemon, salt and spices and make a pickle. Amla and its juice is also used for skin and hair treatments as well as in countless ayurvedic medicines and cosmetics.

52. Giloy

Giloy or Tinospora cordifolia, commonly known as heart-leaved moonseed, is known in Sanskrit as amrutā, meaning the fruit for an eternal life. It is commonly available in the Indian sub-continent and grows very easily, without needing much water or fertile soil. Popular mostly amongst ayurvedic doctors for medicines, giloy, though is not a very common household name. Recently, its demand has increased exponentially because of its immunity boosting properties.

It is a great anti-oxidant, helps to detox the body, purifies blood and reduces the blood sugar level. In a scientific study using human WBCs, the herb helps increasing the killing ability of the macrophages, the resistant cells which aid our body in fighting the foreign antigens.

Giloy can be consumed fresh by taking a small branch, making a powder, or juice and mixing with water. You can also make a kādha by adding tulsi (holy basil), laung (cloves) and adrak (ginger) and drink it. If the fresh plant is not available, Giloy vati tablets are also available in ayurvedic medicine shops or in Patanjali shops.

53. Astragalus

As much as Tulsi is prevalent in Indian history, so is Astragalus popular in the Chinese history. The root of the plant is used for medicinal purposes. It has been used as a herbal medicine for thousands of years in China. It's a unique herb as it possesses adaptogen, i.e. its functionality changes as per the requirement. It is thus, used to cure ailments of heart, blood sugar, hepatitis, respiratory problems, digestive system and seasonal allergy. In traditional Chinese medicine, it has even been used to cure cancer as an alternative treatment to chemotherapy. It is also used cosmetically, for its anti-ageing effects on our skin and boosts immune system.

Astragalus, or Huang Qi in Chinese, has also been used as a traditional herb for curing of covid-19 patients, and is known to have shown promising results. It has anti-viral, as well as anti-inflammatory properties, and has been used widely against earlier outbreak of SARS and Ebola virus. Astragalus has gradually increased its popularity in western countries also because of its adaptogen properties.

54. Munakkā or Dried Grapes

Munakkā is known as the 'Tree of Life" because of its regenerative ability. Munakkās are a dark brown variety of dried grapes with seeds. This variety is mostly used for medicinal properties. It is effective in dry cough and respiratory tract inflammation. Munakkā also helps in checking blood pressure as it increases nitric oxide in blood which widens the narrowing blood vessels.

Roast 7-8 Munakkās in a pan and add rock salt and black pepper to taste. This helps reduce fever and gives strength.

55. Turmeric Powder for Cough

In case of any kind of cough, a simple cure is turmeric powder. Turmeric powder (Haldi) is one of the best antiseptic and antibiotic. Take a quarter to half tea-spoon of turmeric powder and keep it on your tongue just before going bed. It may feel a little dry and spicy initially, but in a few minutes will form like a paste with saliva. Overnight, it will fight the virus and bacteria in the throat region. In 2-3 days, you will feel a major relief in cough or throat pain.

Another method is, you may form small balls (the size of a pea) of turmeric powder and honey. Keep the bottle by your bedside and pop one before going to bed.

56. Lemon Sanitizer

Lemon has been used universally not just for juices or food, but also in soaps, hand wash and dishwashers. Lemon is also used in post meal finger bowls to wash and rinse our hands. It feels fresher than using a liquid hand wash.

Lemon juice has both anti-viral and anti-bacterial properties. In ancient days, when hand sanitizers were unheard of, lemon juice was used to sanitize hands and clothes. We can also spray little lemon juice on our and kids' clothes. It simply doesn't have any side-effects (perhaps may leave a stain). It can also be sprayed a little on table tops, which you may feel slightly sticky though.

57. Warm Lemon Water or Lemon Tea

Add half a lemon to your daily morning glass of warm water throughout the year. Once it's a part of our daily routine, we won't be needing any supplements for Vitamin C. Those who have regular complaints of indigestion, will feel a major improvement in a couple of weeks just by adding this little lemon to your daily routine. Indigestion in the long run is a root cause of numerous disorders of kidney, liver, stomach, intestine and gall bladder as well. Other benefits include reduction in blood LDL cholesterol level and reduce excess body fat. Warm lemon water in the morning is also advised by many gym instructors and dieticians for weight loss. One lemon, multiple benefits.

A tastier substitute to your morning warm lemon water is lemon tea. You can have it instead of your regular bed tea, and may be twice a day. The purpose is an intake of lemon with warm water in the morning before breakfast.

58. Hot Masala Tea / Herbal Tea

Hot masala tea has been effective in prevention as well as curing of mild to moderate cases. Just add little herbs and spices to your daily dose of tea to make it medicinal. Saunth (dry ginger), jaiphal (nutmeg), elaichi (green cardamom), dal chini (cinnamon), laung (cloves), saunf (fennel seeds), kali mirch (black pepper) are some of the commonly available ingredients which you can add to your masala tea according to taste.

Lemon-grass, pudina (mint), tulsi (holy basil), adrak (ginger), rose-petals are other options you can add in your herbal tea. There are various recipes of masala tea and herbal tea with diverse combinations from the above options of ingredients.

59. Hot Milk with Turmeric Powder

Add a pinch of turmeric powder (haldi) to a glass of hot milk and have it daily. It is a complete package of protein, calcium, fat, carbohydrates, vitamins and calories. Turmeric powder is an excellent antibiotic and is used for both external wounds as well for consumption. Paste of turmeric powder has been used for healing all kinds of wounds since ancient times. Intake of hot milk with turmeric fights inner bacteria and virus, aids in rebuilding muscles and bones, gives us strength and is an amazing cure for sore throat and dry cough.

60. Black Tea /Black Coffee

A simple black tea or black coffee without milk and sugar is a better substitute for regular tea and coffee. Its multiple benefits include – it lowers blood sugar levels, aids in weight loss, prevents formation of kidney stones, lowers LDL cholesterol, checks blood pressure of hypertension patients and improves overall heart health.

If pulse of a patient drops below normal, have a cup of black tea or black coffee.

61. Barley Water

Drink one glass of barley water with a pinch of rock salt and one lemon. Barley is also rich in vitamin B, which is found in very low quantity in fruits and vegetables. Barley water improves strength, and can be given in case of weakness. It can also be given to rehydrate the body, as it contains essential vitamin B, vitamin C (lemon) and rock salt. To add to taste, we can add little jaggery instead of sugar.

62. Dates and Almonds

Dates are very popular in middle-east countries for its strength building properties. It is consumed fresh as well as dried. However, in most parts of the world it is sold as a dry-fruit. It is rich in proteins, potassium, iron, magnesium and Vitamin B6. It is also used as a natural sweetener.

Almonds also have similar properties like that of dates, with a rich content of protein, vitamin E, and manganese. Both dates and almonds are known to boost brain efficiency, control blood sugar, LDL cholesterol and blood pressure and are powerful anti-oxidants. Dates, like almonds are also mixed in milk shakes. Both of these make a great snack and are yummier options for strength building and energy for covid-19 patients. Recommended intake is 2-3 dates and 5-6 almonds per day, either taken dry, or soaked overnight, or crushed and mixed with milk. Walnuts and munakkā are also recommended together with almonds, to form a comprehensive supplement.

63. Coconut Water

Coconut water is a natural replacement of the ORS solutions. It contains the essential salts of sodium and potassium. Being available in the natural form, our body absorbs salts more easily from the coconut water than those supplied through supplements. It is especially recommended for patients having diarrhoea. It thus, is considered a natural alternative to glucose drips for rehydration.

Dr. Biswaroop Roy Chowdhury, an internationally acclaimed nutritionist, in his recent book on covid-19 cure, has stressed that the most important ingredient to fight the corona virus is coconut water. He has suggested to drink up to 8 glasses of coconut water in the first day, 4 glasses on the second day and then 2 glasses from there on.

64. Sweat Profusely with Hot Lemon Water

A home remedy, which has been effective for quite a number of people. Boil 2 glasses of water, add one full lemon to it. Now, switch off the fan and air conditioner, and cover yourself with a blanket from head to toe, with just your mouth popping out. Now sip the hot lemon water like your tea. Then lie down and hide inside your blanket for 10 minutes. Allow yourself to sweat profusely. Now remove the blanket and allow your body to cool down. Do not switch on the fans and air conditioner immediately.

This has been very effective in curing fever. If you feel recharged, then you may repeat it again 3-4 times after every 8-12 hours until you have fully recovered.

65. Apply Ghee or Coconut Oil in Nose

Ayurveda has long found cure to illness, which are still unsettling the advanced medical research. Sadly, today the medicines are not ruled by their effectiveness, but by what the giant pharma companies prescribe. There are simple cures and preventions to many ailments, but are not approved by medical research of pharma giants, as they are not profitable options.

The purpose of mentioning it here is not to negate the efforts of pharma companies, but to re-direct the attention of masses to cheaper, proven, age-old practices of Ayurveda, which is within the reach of common man. These practices have proven record of holistic, preventive and curative treatments using natural herbs and plants. Our body easily gets acclimatised to natural products, and have minimal to zero side effects.

Applying coconut oil or ghee is one such ayurvedic preventive and curative measure for nasal ailments. Heat and liquefy ghee or coconut oil and place it in a bowl. Using a dropper, put 2-3 drops of warm oil inside each nostril and press gently. Alternatively, using an index finger, you can simply rub the oil inside each nostril. This helps cleanse the sinuses, lubricates the nose, kills any virus in the nostril or nasal passage. This can be done daily once or twice without any side effects.

66. Lemon Drops in the Nose

There have been unverified claims that putting a drop of lemon juice in your nose can cure a covid-19 patient. Put one drop of lemon juice in each of the nostrils. Lemon juice is also anti-viral. This kills the virus in the nose and throat. It will form a little phlegm in your throat and mouth, just spit it out. After this, gargle with warm saline water, with a few drops of lemon in it, to extract any remaining phlegm in the throat.

Then apply a little coconut oil in both the nostrils. Repeat it for 2-3 days and the results are said to be path breaking.

67. Patanjali Coronil kit

Ayurvedic pharma major, Patanjali has launched Coronil, initially marketed as a cure for Corona. Coronil has had promising results on mild to moderate covid-19 cases. Another reason to cheer is that Coronil is easily available and reasonably priced, whereas commercial medicines preferred by doctors are beyond the affordability (and availability) of a common man.

The complete corona kit contains a couple of more ayurvedic medicines, which are immunity boosters or more like nutrient supplements. The complete dosage includes

a) Divya Swasari Vati – 3 tablets thrice a day with hot water 30 minutes before meal.
b) Patanjali Giloy Ghanvati – 2 tablets thrice a day with hot water 30 minutes after meal.
c) Divya Ashwagandha Ghanvati – 1 tablet thrice a day with hot water 30 minutes after meal.
d) Patanjali Tulsi Ghanvati – 1 tablet thrice a day with hot water 30 minutes after meal.
e) Divya Coronil Tablet – 3 tablets thrice a day with hot water 30 minutes after meal (when Coronil is taken, the above 3 herbs –b, c and d can be avoided as it includes the above 3 herbs too)
f) Divya Anu Taila – put 4-4 drops of Anu Taila on both the nostrils once per day.

68. Arsenicum Album 30 – Homeopathy

The homeopathic medicine, Arsenicum Album 30, was recommended by the ministry of Ayush (Indian health ministry). It is not a cure for the disease, rather is a prophylactic, i.e. it prevents the contraction of covid-19. The same has been distributed in many cities in India by the local municipal corporation.

The recommended dosage is 5 pills at once, empty stomach, for 3 consecutive days. Repeat the dosage every month. Germany is said to have achieved very good recovery rate with various concoctions of homeopathic medicines.

69. Indoor Plants

Our forefathers used to breathe fresh air in their farms, quite in contrast to the way we are breathing in our concrete jungles. Can you feel the difference when you jog through a concrete track, vis-à-vis a walk through the fields? The air we breathe is directly related to how fresh and relaxed we feel.

Culturally, we come from a country, where our ancestors had pots of Tulsi plants in the porch or inside a house and a neem tree in the front garden. These served multiple purposes – eat fresh leaves of Tulsi and neem daily in the morning, natural greenery around us and plenty of oxygen.

Covid-19 patients are constantly monitored for their oxygen saturation levels with ideal situation is a saturation level over 95. We are advised to keep compatible oxygen cylinders in case of emergency. The best natural option is having either a Tulsi plant or areca palm, snake plant, aloe-vera, Gerbera (Orange), neem or orchids. These plants are suitable for indoor pots and are capable of releasing oxygen 24 hours a day. It is because, these plants have the ability to perform a photosynthesis called Crassulacean Acid Metabolism (CAM), which continues even at night.

Therefore, these indoor plants assist us in maintaining our oxygen saturation levels.

70. Antiviral Herbs

All the medicines that are or were being researched upon have their roots in some or the other natural herbs. Ayurveda has a rich history of herbs, which is said to possess cure to almost all the diseases ever known to mankind. However, over generations the ayurvedic practitioners have declined. More so, because of the influence of the pharmaceutical giants, who have twisted the medical fraternity into believing that only the medicines prescribed by researches of giant pharmaceutical companies can relieve a human from pain and diseases.

The reliance on generations old Ayurvedic, Homeopathic, Chinese and Persian (Iranian) traditional treatments have lost their reverence. Here's a compilation of a few anti-viral herbs, which have been used in various concoctions to cure viral diseases:

a) Holy Basil (Tulsi)
b) Oregano
c) Garlic (Lehsun)
d) Ginger (Adrak)
e) Amla (Avla)
f) Fennel (Saunf)
g) Cardamom (Moti elaichi)
h) Sage plant
i) Indian Bay Leaf (Tejpatta)
j) Fresh Turmeric (Kachi haldi)
k) Cloves (Laung)

l) Black pepper (Kali mirch)
m) Cinnamon (Dal chini)
n) Dried Raisins (Munakkā)
o) Lemon Balm
p) Peppermint (Pudina)
q) Rosemary (Gulmehendi)
r) Echinacea purpurea (purple coneflower)
s) Sambucus
t) Liquorice
u) Astragalus
v) Ginseng
w) Dandelion
x) Fenugreek seeds (Methi)
y) Curry leaves

VIII. Basic Medication

The best practice is to consult a doctor and start taking prescribed medicines. However, there are a few basic OTC medicines, which are being prescribed by doctors as a must have at home for precautionary measures. Some medicines may be banned in some countries, as per the respective food and drug policies. Most medicines mentioned below are as per Indian regulations.

Recommended dosage may vary from patient to patient. However, even for the same patient, the dosage can vary as per different doctors' diagnosis.

71. Home Care Vs Hospitals

Hospitals are always a safer option for covid-19 patients, for they are under constant observation by a team of doctors for any medical emergency. In the current scenario, there are more patients in every city than the available beds in the hospitals. There are make-shift hospitals, with tens of beds and ventilators lined up in marriage halls and convention centres. So, here an important question is, how necessary it is to get admitted in a hospital?

For covid-19 patients, monitoring two vital parameters are necessary, temperature and oxygen saturation levels. For diabetic and hypertension patients, daily monitoring of blood pressure and blood sugar levels are also mandatory. If fever persists between 99°F to 102°F and oxygen saturation levels are over 95, then medication can be continued from home. 80-90% of the patients recover with mild to moderate symptoms of covid-19. Hence, they do not require hospitalization. Only the remaining, especially those who have other pre-existing diseases have higher chances of complexities. Many doctors are also offering online consultancy so that the patients do not have to venture out to clinics and spread the virus.

Home care also ensures that the patient is close to his family members and continue to get emotional support. In case of hospitals, patients' relatives are not allowed even inside the campus of hospitals, which is emotionally draining. However, in case of home-care, it is very imperative to maintain complete isolation of patients, to check the spread of virus.

72. PPE Kit for the Attendant

In case of home care, it is the foremost responsibility of the patient and his family members that the patient is put in complete isolation. Only one member of a family looks after serving or monitoring the patient. Maintaining total hygiene is the duty of the person. He must wear a PPE kit (Personal Protective Equipment) before entering the room of the patient. In case a full PPE is unavailable at that time, alternative option can be a face mask, a face shield (can be made with a hairband and toughened plastic), shower cap, hand gloves, a full body raincoat and socks.

Whenever you leave the room, do not touch anything else, but enter a washroom straightaway and sanitise yourself. The patient will need an emotional need to talk to someone. It must be done remotely via an audio or video call only.

73. Monitor Body Temperature

Keep a digital thermometer handy (or an analog will also do). If you have a slight fever, keep a record of temperatures every 4-6 hours. The record will help you and the physicians identify a temperature pattern or symptoms to diagnose the cause of fever. It could be due to covid-19 or just seasonal flu, dengue, malaria or any other viral fever. Do not share the thermometers, and sanitise it after every use.

74. Paracetamol

Paracetamol is one of the most commonly available OTC medicines. These are mostly prescribed for fever, headache and body ache. A few of them are also prescribed for common cold and cough. Some of the commonly available paracetamols you can keep at your place are: Dolo 650, Calpol, Crocin, Saridon, etc. Dosage may depend on the temperature and age. For an adult, 500 to 650 mg tablets can be taken up to thrice a day (after meal) with a minimum gap of 5-6 hours. In case of high fever, doctors may also give up to 4000 mg of paracetamol per adult per day.

However, such heavy dosage needs to be medically monitored and may have side effects like an upset stomach or stress our liver.

75. HCQ

HCQs or Hydroxy Chloroquine is one of the first medicines that was known to be effective against the covid-19 virus. It is more popularly known as anti-malarial drug, as earlier it was widely used in treating malaria. HCQ is currently prescribed by most of the doctors in India for covid-19 cases. In western countries too, it was very much in demand. However, recently some countries have refrained from using HCQs stating low recovery rates of patients. Common HCQs available in the market are HCQ-200, HCQS 200, HCQS 400, Lariago, etc. It is a commonly available prescription drug, to be taken in consultation with doctors only.

The normal prescribed dosage for adults is 2 tablets of 200 mg per day, one each in morning and night after meal. As the dosage is heavy, few doctors also recommend having milk twice a day to avoid side-effects, or taking a tablet to prevent acidity.

76. Vitamin C

It is imperative to enhance intake of fresh fruits and vegetables for Vitamins and other essential nutrients. In the short run, doctors are also advising taking supplements to boost your immunity and fight virus in the early stages. Normal requirement for an adult is 1000 mg of vitamin C per day. So doctors, recommend 2 tablets of 500 mg each per day (one morning, one evening after meal).

Generally prescribed supplements for Vitamin C is Tab Limcee 500 or an equivalent.

77. Vitamin D

Vitamin D is easily available from the morning sunlight. However, it's not very common in fruits and vegetables. So, a shorter route is supplements like – Calciquick D3, Urays D3 60k, Tab Shelcal. Recommended dosage is one tablet of 60,000 units per week. For patients with weakness, the dosage may be increased to 1 tablet per day, for 4 consecutive days, followed by one each per week.

78. Vitamin B

Vitamin B is available in low quantity in fruits and vegetables. Options are wholegrains, dairy products, legumes, citrus fruits and bananas. Then animal foods such as eggs, meat, beef, fish, etc. So supplements for Vitamin B complex or Vitamin B12 are easily available OTC. These supplements are safe to be taken every day (in quantity as prescribed by your physician), normally 1 tablet per day. Commonly available tablets include Becosule, B Tab, etc.

79. Zinc

Zinc is less popular among the supplements commonly suggested for immunity builder. However, in covid-19 times, zinc supplement has been strongly suggested by the medical fraternity. As per Dr. Soumitra Das, director south Asia – Zinc Nutrient Initiative, zinc is proven to be effective at slowing the rate of replication of virus such as corona virus, SARS and common cold in our body. The zinc requirement of our body is just 8-11 mgs per day for proper functioning of immune system and enzymes. But is less commonly available in our regular food diet. Common zinc supplements are Tab Zincovit, Zinconia-50, Zinc Sulphate, or Z&D DS 20.

80. Antibiotics

Antibiotics for sore-throat has also known to be effective in fighting virus at initial stages, until it has penetrated our lungs. Commonly prescribed antibiotics are Azithral, Azimax, Azithromycin, Azee 500, etc. It is advisable to take a 5 days' course (1 pill per day 30 minutes before dinner) of antibiotics for effective results. HCQs along with azithromycin in combination, is today the most recommended treatment for covid-19 in India. Rest of the medicines suggested are just multivitamin supplements or due to comorbidity or to prevent acidity.

81. In Case of Breathlessness

In very selective cases, doctors are also recommending Tab Dexona 5mg. These are suggested in case of shortness of breath. It contains steroids, and there are chances of increase in blood sugar levels. So for diabetic patients, daily monitoring of blood sugar is very important. This is a strictly prescription drug, to be taken under advise of doctors only.

82. For Heartburn and Acid Reflux

The combination of HCQs and azithromycin is a strong dosage and may have certain side-effects. Acidity is one of the most common of them. So, it is recommended to take antacids or similar pills to prevent acidity, like Rantac-D, Omex D, Pantocid, Pantosec D, etc.

Recommended dosage for adults is either just one tablet per day, or one in morning and one in evening before meal.

83. Cough Syrup

One of the foremost symptoms of covid-19 is dry cough or sore throat. In the initial stages the virus spreads only in the mouth, nasal passage and throat, before reaching the lungs in the 5th to 6th day. A cough syrup may not be an effective shield against virus, but it aids the body in fighting the virus, and cures dry cough and mild fever. Commonly available syrups are Syp. Bro-zedex, Syp Benadryl, etc.

84. For Running Nose / Throat pain

Running nose or sneezing is the worst spreader of virus. If one has a running nose, foremost precaution necessary is covering the face with a mask or handkerchief, and strictly take care that the handkerchief is washed separately with a disinfectant and not mixed with other clothes.

Medications for running nose are Montelukast (Singulair), Tab Cetrizine-10 mg, Tab Wikoryl, Vicks vaporub, Tab Vicks action 500, etc.

85. Betadine for Mouthwash & Gargle

It helps kill germs and virus in the mouth and throat and prevents infections. It's easy to use and easily available. Pour the syrup in a cup and mix with warm water. Swish part of the solution briefly in the mouth, gargle in your mouth and spit it out. May repeat it 2-4 times a day or as directed by physician.

Alternate options for gargle are lukewarm salt water; warm water with a pinch of salt and few drops of lemon; warm water with a pinch of turmeric powder; or water boiled with tea leaves, like black tea with no other ingredients.

86. ORS solutions

Oral rehydration salt, popularly known as ORS solutions like Electral powder are recommended by WHO (World Health Organisation) for replenishment of body vitals in case of illness. During diarrhoea or loose motions, our body gets dehydrated and also loses vital nutrients and minerals. Our body gets weaker. ORS solutions enables drinking a lot of water and replenishes essential sugar and salts of sodium and potassium.

WHO recommended ORS are cheap and easily available OTC (Over the counter) in a pharmacy. Alternatively, make one at home. Add 6 teaspoons of sugar, half tea-spoon of salt to 1 litre of drinking water. Adults can drink half-a litre to 1 litre per day to rehydrate the body. Other options to rehydrate are Glucon-C, Glucon-D, lemon water, or fresh juices.

87. Pulse Oximeter

How to check if your body is fighting well against the virus or getting tired. Apart from temperature, another thing you need to monitor is blood oxygen saturation levels. It is because, the first organs that the virus attack are our lungs. For an average adult Indian, oxygen levels above 95 are normal. However, if the level drops below 90, you may need an external oxygen support and should immediately consult a doctor. An optimum way to check oxygen level is, first sit in a calm position, take a deep breath and put the oximeter on your index finger. Alternatively, take a 5 minutes' walk in your room and then check the oxygen levels. If oxygen level is between 90 to 95, perform deep breathing for 3-5 minutes, 3-4 times a day. It starkly improves oxygen saturation levels.

88. Portable Oxygen Cylinder

A portable oxygen cylinder (the size of large perfume bottles) is now easily available in pharmaceutical shops. If your blood oxygen levels drop below 90 and hospitals are not in close vicinity, it is advisable to keep a stock of 1-2 such bottles for emergency. The hospitals are already short of beds, so keeping stock of oxygen is always a good choice.

A similar option is portable oxygen concentrator (POC). It is easy to use at home and is easily available both online and offline. This can be used in case of shortness of breath or low oxygen levels in consultation with doctors. These are considered to be very safe to use. Caution must be taken, if it is worn while sleeping, as our breathing pattern changes while we are asleep.

IX. A Doctor knows the best

It is unfortunate that many doctors these days are contradicting any diagnosis by other doctors, or the suggested treatment or the recommended dosage. It is therefore, highly advised to trust one doctor and follow his treatment, as multiple advice may add to confusion.

89. Consult a Doctor

India is an abode of home remedies, where the worst of diseases is known to have been cured by granny prescribed medicines. I too am a big advocate of home remedies and avoid medicines to the extent, that my body really needs them to come out of pain or disease. Covid-19, however, has foxed grannies and doctors equally across the globe. No doctor can guarantee to save you if the virus spreads badly in your body, but doctors can definitely help, if there are slightest of chances. Your vitals can be tested and necessary medications can be suggested. So don't hesitate in consulting a doctor for your life.

90. Check Nearby Hospitals

The toughest question I faced was whether to visit a doctor or not. Hospitals everywhere are packed only with covid-19 patients. In a situation, when you are having mild symptoms and unsure if it is a viral fever or covid-19, what should we do? Should we visit a doctor, or a hospital and risk coming in contact with another infected patient?

One option is to consult the doctors online and monitor the symptoms. Meanwhile, check the availability of beds in nearby hospitals. Due to shortage of beds, there are also multiple makeshift hospitals, with beds lined up in multi-purpose halls. If you have a helping hand at home, it is advisable to consult doctors online. Keep track of hospitals with ventilator facilities, with some back-up options, if the rooms get occupied. If you are alone, you shouldn't try to manage it by yourself and immediately get admitted to a nearby hospital.

91. List of Allergies and Medical History

Covid-19 has had maximum impact on patients with comorbidity. Especially those having cancer, heart ailments, diabetes, kidney or liver ailments have a slower recovery rate. You may have recovered from one such medical condition. Still, if you have had a medical history with anyone of the above, kindly disclose it to your doctors along with other medications already running. The dosage will be advised accordingly. Also remember to list, any allergies you may have.

92. Blood Tests Recommended by Doctors

Monitoring the vitals are of utmost importance to diagnose the current condition of the patient. So, our blood is investigated thoroughly to answer the questions of the doctors. The common ones requested by doctors are:

a) CBC
b) ESR
c) Creatinine
d) CRP
e) RBS
f) SGPT
g) Ferritin
h) LDH
i) Electrolytes
j) D-Dimer
k) IL-6

93. Chest X-Ray & CT Scan

The primary organs that the corona virus attack are our lungs. So it's important to monitor how deep the virus has spread. One of the primary reports that a doctor will need, is either, or both of these

a) Chest x-ray,
b) HRCT-Chest-Lungs

Though, the tests should be done in consultation with the doctors only. In small towns there are paucity of CT scan machines. It is only advisable to keep track of test centers in your town, so you can visit them as and when required.

94. Update Yourself About Critical Medicines

I am glad to know that none of your family members are yet infected with a virus. If not, that means you have already won one battle against the virus. You are already more knowledgeable and experienced than me, and chances of you reading this book are low. Others should know that being prepared in advance greatly increases your chances of winning the war.

Doctors are over-burdened, there are shortage of medicines. So, a gentle tip, read a little about the common medicines used for treatment of covid-19 and prepare yourself for any emergency. Here's a list of common medicines required in case of critical illness.

a) HCQs or Hydroxy Chloroquine: It is commonly advised today in India for mild to moderate symptoms. However, globally there have been mixed reviews in its effectiveness.

b) Favipiravir / Fabiflu: manufactured and marketed by Glenmark India, Fabiflu is the first medicine which got regulatory approval for treatment of covid-19 patients. It has shown promising results in treatment of mild to moderate cases.

c) Inj. Tocilizumab: Injection Tocilizumab by Cipla is the most highly sought-after medicine today. It is an immune-suppressant and has been approved temporarily by the government for investigational therapy. This is used only on critical patients to fight respiratory distress immune complications and has been able to save critical lives. However, if dosage or timing of admission of injection is not monitored perfectly, it may cause adverse complications.

d) Inj Remdesivir: Injection Remdesivir, is manufactured and marketed by Cipla (Cipremi) and Hetero Healthcare (Covifor) in India. It is an only drug approved by USFDA in treatment of critical cases of covid-19

95. Check Availability of Medicines

Doctors in different parts of the world have varied opinions about effectiveness of medicines. In our country, the medicines used widely by doctors are already in acute supply with soaring prices. Once a news or research is out about a medicine to be more effective than others in treating covid-19, its demand increases exponentially and suddenly there is a severe shortage of the drug. So, it only makes sense to remain abreast with the current medicines and three alternate sources of availability in case of an emergency.

Injections like Tocilizumab and Remdesivir are very effective in saving covid-19 patients if used at the right time, neither early, nor late. These are in high demand, acute supply and the sale is monitored by government. Every sale is mandated with the covid-19 status of the patient, the HRCT scan and recommendation of the medical team of respective hospital. Currently, there are only two suppliers – Cipla and Hetero Healthcare. If you have any contacts in the respective companies or government authorities, check with them the availability and requisite documentation for procuring the same. Further, you may consult with your physician for alternate medication in case of an emergency.

96. Ventilator Support

What is a ventilator and what is its importance in covid-19 times? In layman's terms, a ventilator does the breathing work for a patient, when the lungs are not working optimally. Covid-19 is a respiratory disease which infects our lungs. When our lungs are underperforming, there is a shortage of oxygen in blood. Separate oxygen cylinders are required to supply pure oxygen to enhance oxygen saturation levels. But as the infection increases, our lungs are not able to intake the oxygen supply. Thus, ventilator support is required, which does the breathing for us, when our lungs get weaker.

An external oxygen support is required in only 10-15% cases. As the recovery rates across the globe are improving, the percentage of people requiring extra oxygen is declining. Ventilator support again gets down to 2-5% of the patients, especially in the cases of comorbidity. Currently, there are numerous make-shift hospitals in every city. However, not all of them are equipped with ventilators, required in case of an emergency. So choose the hospitals with ventilator facilities, if the need to get admitted arise.

97. Plasma Therapy

It is technically referred to as Convalescent Plasma Therapy (CPT). CPT is a procedure where the plasma, from a covid-19 recovered patient, is transferred to an active covid-19 patient. Our blood is composed of plasma, the liquid; and WBCs, RBCs and Platelets, combined to form the particles. When a foreign antigen enters our body, the anti-bodies (protein) present in our plasma identifies them and attacks to destroy them. Thus, keeping our body free from any diseases.

In certain cases, it takes our body a little time in identifying the antigen (bacteria or virus) and forming the respective anti-body to fight the virus. This could be due to low immunity or due to other pre-existing diseases, which has already weakened our anti-bodies. In the said time, the antigen or virus attacks the body and infects our organs. It's like an on-going war inside our body. The moment our antibodies lose the war, we perish.

So, doctors have devised a plan to support our army of anti-bodies, i.e. give them a detailed knowledge about the virus they are fighting. This external support is given in the form of convalescent plasma, which contains the anti-bodies who have already defeated the virus once. This convalescent plasma educates the anti-bodies of the recipient patient, on how to kill the enemy, and helps them win the war.

Currently, multiple medical research centres are experimenting on treating covid-19 patients with CPT, and have treated critical patients with a fair amount of success. However, doctors are still understanding if there could be any side effects or allergies of the same.

98. Is Vaccine Out Yet?

A vaccine works somewhat in a similar way as above. In a vaccination or immunization process, a weakened dosage of antigen is injected in a person. The person's antibodies react to the foreign element and nullifies the virus. In doing so, our body develops the respective anti-body to shield the body against the same virus in future. The immunity may last from a few months to a lifetime. So accordingly, some vaccinations are required to be taken again after a certain period to continue the immunity.

Till the date, the book was published, there has been no confirmed news of any vaccine against the novel corona virus, out in the market. Though there are tens of companies already claiming to have been successful in formulating a vaccine. The same are said to be in different stages of trial or government approval. Here's a list of a few companies you may want to track the progress of:

1) Gamaleya Institute, Russia: It is expected to be the first institute to receive the government approval for public use of the vaccine. The company is expected to start the phase 3 or final phase of trials on August 3. It is thus expected to receive the approval for public use in mid-august, i.e. before completion of phase 3 trials.

2) Serum Institute of India: Currently, the most promising results of a vaccine undergoing final trials are that of the team from Oxford University, UK and a British pharmaceutical company AstraZeneca. Pune based Serum Institute of India, world's largest vaccine manufacturer, has collaborated with Oxford-AstraZeneca to manufacture 1 billion vials of their vaccine. 100 million doses are expected to be ready by the time the final approval is received.

3) Serum Institute of India: Serum Institute is also conducting phase 3 trials for another vaccine, a BCG candidate VPM1002 which is showing promising results in trials.

4) SK Bioscience, South Korea: This company has again collaborated with Oxford-AstraZeneca to manufacture their vaccine.

5) Moderna Inc., USA: It has initiated the phase 3 trials and the results are expected in December.

6) Pfizer USA: Pfizer has collaborated with German firm BioNTech for development of a vaccine against the novel corona virus SARS-CoV-2, which causes covid-19. Its vaccine belongs to a different category, known as messenger RNA vaccine. These involve modification of a messenger RNA to make the cells recreate the spike of the SARS-CoV-2 virus. Thus, it aids in identification of the similar SARS-CoV-2 virus to attack. It is already in late stage trials, and is expected to get the approvals by October end.

7) Covaxin, India: Indigenously developed by Bharat Biotech in collaboration with Indian Council of Medical Research (ICMR) and National Institute of Virology (NIV), it is in the initial stages of human trials.

8) Others in fray: CanSino Biologics, China; Cadila, India; Serum Institute of India in collaboration with Codagenix, New York; Indian Immunologicals Ltd with Griffith University of Australia; and Gennova, India are some of the other entities under different stages of trials. Currently, there are 25 vaccines globally undertaking human trials with 139 more vaccines in pre-clinical trial stage.

99. Herd Immunity

Herd immunity is achieved when a large percentage of the population is immune to the virus. It can be achieved by two ways: one is by vaccination, and the second is when a sizable population has recovered from the illness and developed anti-bodies.

In both these cases, there are chances that a person may get infected with the virus. However, his anti-bodies will eventually weaken and kill the virus. In the meanwhile, he can though transmit the weakened version of the virus to those he comes in contact with. When a person, who has no prior exposure to the virus, is infected with the weakened version of the virus, then his body is in a better position to fight and survive the virus.

There have been various theories to herd immunity, as there have been no formal case of a government actively promoting herd immunity. One such theory was to ask all the high risk people to stay inside their respective homes, including kids, elderly people, persons with comorbidity, like diabetes, asthma, cancer patients to patients with any respiratory disorders. The low risk people getting infected with virus will have a higher recovery rate. Also any transmission from a person with strong immunity will be a weakened version of the virus. This will enable faster recovery of even the persons with lower immunity. This will improve overall recovery rate and hence may gradually lead to eradication of the virus.

This theory still comes with a lot of risk, and a government cannot risk human lives in order to experiment a trend, which has not been tried before.

100. Ask Questions to Your Doctors?

Apart from the aforementioned conventional and non-conventional treatment, there are tons of treatment methodologies we hear every day. Keep yourself updated. Here are a few FAQs people may have.

a) Is it safe to participate in clinical trials of a vaccine?
   Yes, mostly they are. In clinical trials, first the pharma companies screen the participants and select healthy patients who have no other ailments. Second, the human trials start only after they have shown positive results on animal trials including apes. Third, the dosage is kept mild for safety.

b) Can home-care or late admission to hospitals be risky?
   Yes, it can be, if the vitals are not monitored periodically. In case of slightest of doubts, consult the doctors immediately.

c) Can getting a covid-19 test be risky?
   May be. Basic precautions are to be taken while getting yourself tested. There have been cases, where the first test results have been negative and positive later. It can be attributed to late boost of virus. It has also been referred, that initially the patients may have been suffering with viral fever or malaria, and said to have contracted the virus only at the crowded test centres.

d) Is current genre of medicines effective in treating covid-19?
   There is currently no approved drug for treatment of this disease. The medicines used are all under different stages of experiments which may have been effective on certain patients. Our own defence mechanism is the primary basis for survival or death of a person. If the immunity is very low, the chances of a person recovering only with support of medications is very low.

X. Religious and Non-Conventional Healing techniques

Our body is made up of five *Tatvas,* namely physical body (skin, muscles and bones), mental body (emotions), Breath body (breath), Energy body (life force), and bliss body (Our essence). Our medical science, physical work-out and *yoga āsanas* focuses on our physical body. Through *pranayama* or breathing exercises, we can control our breath body. Meditation helps us control our mental body. The techniques of maintaining our energy body is rooted in our Vedic science and includes Reiki, colour therapy, aroma therapy, touch therapy, acupressure, acupuncture, cellular healing and advanced meditation. The skill required to control our bliss body is long lost encrypted in Vedas. It is believed to be practiced by our ancient sages, and assisted them to observe things beyond the dimensions of space and time.

101. Chanting Aum

The frequency of Aum is exactly the same as the frequency of earth's rotation around its own axis. Every religion uses some or other forms of Aum as their holy word, Om, Omkar, Amen, āmin, and Shalom. Aum chanting is advocated for both physical and metaphysical healing of body and mind.

'Aum' or 'Om' chanting is one of the oldest sacred practices of the universe. As per the Hindu Vedas, it is known to possess all the vibrations of the universe and is known to have extraordinary spiritual power. There has been numerous research on effects of aum chanting on human mind, body, and society (when aum chanting has been done with masses).

As per a research paper from MIT college of engineering, Pune, India, "Survey on Om meditation: its effects on the human body and Om meditation as a tool for stress management", daily practice of Aum mantra helps in increasing the level of human attention and concentration, stabilization of brain, and increase of energy.

102. Meditation

Meditation is a universally accepted technique of consciously controlling your mind and body by sitting calmly with eyes closed. There are many ways to meditate. You can sit with your eyes closed in a quiet room and concentrate on one focal point, a thought, an activity or an object. Some may also prefer to play some soothing music to help them focus on their body and prevent any wandering thoughts.

Advanced stages of meditation allow us to focus on body parts one by one, control our breath and heart-beat and even feel our organs. Emotionally it helps us to relax our mind, evade anxiety or depression, treat any psychological disorder and ensure positive thoughts. This is especially important in times of isolation, as quarantine periods have been found to be emotionally very depressing. Patients in hospitals are not allowed to meet any of their family members, not even see from a distance. More than physical, it has been an emotional challenge for patients to recover from solitude.

Physically, meditation has soothed patients with hypertension, heart ailments and diabetes. High blood pressure or hypertension, as the name suggests, is a physical ailment caused by anxiety and mental pressure. Positively controlled mind ensures a healthy heart and an improved hormonal balance. Focussed breathing with meditation ensures a healthy pair of lungs. Thus, meditation is a recommended technique for not just prevention and cure of covid-19, but for every person on the planet to ensure harmony.

103. Live Your Hobby

Lockdown and isolation is either one of the most challenging phases of life, or has been the most beautiful. In any case, it is far from our routine life. It is a change we have to consciously adapt to. It is a period to do things, we have never done before. The initial lockdown days for me seemed like a life in prison. Soon, it was about enjoying the extra me-time, family time, taking out my bucket list and ticking out my hobbies.

For others, it has been about going back to the drawing board, revisiting the business models, or adventuring a start-up. It is all about looking at the greener side. News and social media is filled with updates on celebrities and our relatives losing the battle with covid-19. We have a choice to either give up, or learn some music, read some books, catch up on movies and play our favourite sport. What is it you wanna do, before you die?

104. Reiki

'Rei' means 'universal life', 'Ki' means 'energy'. Reiki is a practice of healing self or others by using universal energy. The method to heal, by channelizing energy, was discovered by Dr. Mikao Usui of Japan. Reiki can be given by a Reiki healer by putting both the palms on the diseased part of the patient. The Reiki masters can though, heal a patient even from vast distances across continents.

There have been no registered cases of a patient recovering from Covid-19 only with Reiki treatment. However, Reiki treatment is more like a belief in religion. Thousands of Reiki masters across the globe have been productively giving Reiki treatments to treat mild ailments, as well as to expedite recovery along with regular medicines.

Reiki healing can be learned by anyone from a Reiki master, irrespective of any religion. It has no side-effects, and can never be used to cause harm to anybody. For advanced healing, there are also symbols for three stages of practice. There is also a procedure of attunement, performed by Reiki masters to relay the energy channels. After attunement, a person becomes a Reiki channel, who can channelize universal energy for healing purposes.

105. Nārāyana Jaap

A Nārāyana jaap is another form of spiritual healing, or can be considered as a Hindu version of Reiki. The best part is that the healing process can be performed by anyone. It is based on Hindu religion, where the name of the supreme lord, Nārāyana, is chanted to bless the receiver with healing energy. Similarly, it can be performed by a person of any religion by meditating religiously, chanting the name of the lord you pray to, and blessing the desired person.

It is imperative that the recipient of the blessings believes in the cosmic healing powers. For minor ailments like fever, common cold, body ache, there have been miraculous results with an instant relief. Even in chronic illness, it has aided in speedy recovery. The procedure can be repeated daily until the recovery of the sick patient. Notably, this technique can be performed from any place for a recipient sitting miles away, and has no side-effects whatsoever on the patron.

There are many variations of this technique, commonly known as Nārāyana Reiki, and can be learned under a trainer in your area. A simple technique which can be effectively performed at home is as follows, imagine that the holy grace of lord is healing the patient. Say 'Nārāyana Nārāyana', followed by Chanting 'Ram' 108 times, then 56 times, then 21 times, then again 'Nārāyana Nārāyana'.

Another way is, imagine the child form of the patient in your lap, put your one hand on his third eye, and other hand on his root chakra. Thank the lord and pray for his well-being. Chant 'Nārāyana' and 'Ram' in the above mentioned procedure. Repeat it by putting the second hand on all the other chakras. There are also symbols for advanced levels of healing.

The key to healing is meditation, gratitude, belief that cosmic energy possesses the healing powers, and a devoted prayer in the name of lord.

106. Acupressure

Acupressure is a form of alternate medical treatment by pressing the acupoints on the body's meridians. It is based on the principal of life force energy flowing through our meridians, and applying pressure on the acupoints to clear any blockages in those meridians. It is believed that all the acupoints of the meridians are present on both of our palms and soles. There are more than 75 different acupoints on our palms for different parts and organs of our body. Apart from these, there are also pressure points on different parts of our body for respective ailments.

The techniques of hand reflexology, or massage therapy uses the same principal as that of acupressure. In ancient times, the principles of acupressure were used in ayurvedic and traditional Chinese healing techniques. It was practiced in kung-fu as well, to disarm or knock out an enemy and render him unconscious by striking a meridian.

There are no particular acupoints to prevent us from any virus. However, acupressure helps us fight the initial symptoms of the disease, viz. fever, throat infection, running nose, diarrhoea and breathing issues, by clearing the blockages in the respective meridians. This aids us in quicker recovery.

107. Colour Therapy

Colour Therapy or Chromo therapy is a healing technique by looking at a particular colour; or directing colour ray to a relevant body part; or making colour coded dots on our palms and fingers with a pen; or wrapping a body part with an applicable coloured cloth. A common place where we experience colour therapy are spa centres and salons. The ambience is created using chromo therapy and aroma therapy to relax our body and mind. These colours helps us to balance our chakras.

The 7 chakras or energy centres present on our body are represented by 7 different colours. Our chakras are located on our back, facing towards frontal side and exact locations are as follows:

a) Crown / *Sahastra Chakra* (Top of head)   Violet Colour
b) Third eye / *Agya Chakra* (Between the eyes)   Indigo Colour
c) Throat / *Vishudha Chakra* (Throat)   Blue Colour
d) Heart / *Anahat Chakra* (Centre chest)   Green Colour
e) Solar Plexus / *Manipur Chakra* (Stomach)   Yellow Colour
f) Sacral / *Svadhisthana Chakra*
   (Just above pubic bone)   Orange Colour
g) Root / *Muladhar Chakra*
   (Near tailbone of spine)   Red Colour

Balance of chakras ensures an equilibrium of energy in our body. This helps us to monitor our body vitals, hormonal balance and a calm state of mind.

108. Cellular Healing

All the cells of our body die and get replaced by new cells. There are about 50 to 75 trillion cells in our body, which live from a few hours to a few years. The nucleus of the dying cells passes on all the memories and information to the new cell, ranging from our childhood memories, eye colour, genetic and biological information. The old damaged cells are replaced by new ones. Our wounds get healed by the same principle. A liver transplant works with the similar concept. Some reptiles like lizard can regrow a limb, human genes haven't yet mastered the genetic code for that.

Cellular healing and cellular regeneration are two very similar concepts. Dr Deepak Chopra has done intensive work in cellular healing via deep meditation, to concentrate at cellular level. It prevents diseased patterns from passing on, enabling replication of only healthy new cells.

A guide to practice self-cellular healing can be found in the book, 'The Journey', by Brandon Bays.

Hope

There is no greater strength than 'Hope'. Nobody has ever seen god, but a belief exists, that somewhere a supernatural power is overlooking all of us and rewarding us for all our good deeds. A prayer gives us all, the strength we need to believe that we can survive. Man may have mastered millions of techniques to govern the universe. We still need to learn to control our innermost fears of death and extinction. All we need, is a leap of faith, that we will survive, prosper and together give humanity its real meaning.

Destiny means that the moment of our birth and death is pre-destined. We cannot live a moment beyond that, nor can anyone kill us before that. We can only control the moment of truth, i.e. now, and choose the way we want to live. So let us all pray, "God, we have whole-heartedly accepted the universe that you have given us. What you have created is adequate to meet all our needs, but we still crave for more. We know that death is inevitable, still we desire for eternity. Our quest to remain happy and not just alive is what makes us different from other animals. Thank you lord for all that you have given us. Today onwards, we all will strive to stay alive, be joyful and shower a few smiles along the way."

Closing Note

The above 108 ways are all important in their own respect. I will still add some recommendations on "Must Do", based on hundreds of feedback I received.

a) The 3 *pranayamas,* namely Bhastrikā, Kapāl-bhāti and Anulom-vilom are must for prevention as well for recovery. It also improves the most important oxygen levels.

b) Coconut water and sweet lime (Mosambi) juice is vital for rehydration and essential nutrients, prevents weakness.

c) Continue taking kādha and turmeric (haldi) milk for immunity building and as an anti-viral.

d) If you have any illness symptoms, do keep oximeter to monitor your oxygen levels.

e) Primary medications for home-care are paracetamol, antibiotic, Vitamin C, Vitamin D, Vitamin B, Zinc and an antacid.

f) Self-isolation is mandatory to prevent the virus from spreading to your family and friends, especially elders and kids.

Bibliography

1. _https://www.mohfw.gov.in/pdf/MindingourmindsduringCoronaedit edat.pdf_
2. _https://www.forbes.com/sites/benjaminlaker/2020/03/13/how-to-be-positive-in-the-coronavirus-world/#6f2cd2cf3450_
3. _https://www.bbc.com/news/world-asia-india-53485039_
4. _https://www.betterhealth.vic.gov.au/health/healthyliving/cycling-health-benefits_
5. _https://www.livescience.com/12951-10-infectious-diseases-ebola-plague-influenza.html_
6. _https://food.ndtv.com/health/8-incredible-benefits-of-astragalus-root-for-health-and-beauty-1667068_
7. _https://www.1mg.com/ayurveda/munakka-78_
8. _https://www.healthline.com/nutrition/black-tea-benefits_
9. _https://health.economictimes.indiatimes.com/news/industry/zinc-can-play-pertinent-role-in-mitigating-covid-19-dr-soumitra-das/75583522_
10. _https://www.healthline.com/nutrition/antiviral-herbs_
11. _https://www.ecofriendlylink.com/blog/best-juices-for-diabetics/_
12. _https://www.ncbi.nlm.nih.gov/pmc/articles/PMC6571565/_
13. _https://www.healthline.com/nutrition/vitamin-b-foods_
14. _https://www.1mg.com/otc/electral-powder-otc135154_
15. _https://patient.info/news-and-features/covid-19-how-to-treat-coronavirus-at-home_
16. _https://www.thehindu.com/news/cities/mumbai/placebo-effect-untested-homoeopathy-drug-being-distributed-widely/article31645532.ece_
17. _https://www.livemint.com/news/world/remdesivir-dexamethasone-hydroxychloroquine-new-studies-clarify-what-drugs-help-hurt-for-covid-19-treatment-11595166764281.html_
18. _https://gallery-repo.inshorts.com/gallery/view/a9535dee-32a5-4fca-96d7-2e8c312efdcd_
19. _https://www.hopkinsmedicine.org/health/wellness-and-prevention/types-of-complementary-and-alternative-medicine_

20. https://www.mind.org.uk/information-support/drugs-and-treatments/complementary-and-alternative-therapies/list-of-complementary-alternative-therapies/

21. https://juniperpublishers.com/nfsij/NFSIJ.MS.ID.555572.php#:~:text=As%20is%20evident%20from%20the,12.41%25)%2C%20moisture%20(18.34%25)

22. https://www.drbronner.com/all-one-blog/2019/10/ayurvedic-uses-coconut-oil/#:~:text=1.)&text=Benefits%3A%20improved%20circulation%2C%20lymph%20massage,and%20aids%20in%20better%20sleep.

23. https://wiki.nurserylive.com/t/top-9-plants-that-absorb-co2-at-night-as-well-best-for-indoors/315

24. https://www.clinicaltrialsarena.com/news/glenmark-fabiflu-trial-data/

25. https://timesofindia.indiatimes.com/life-style/health-fitness/health-news/covid-19-treatment-experts-worry-excessive-usage-of-tocilizumab-remdesivir-can-do-more-harm-than-good/photostory/76939986.cms

26. https://www.businessinsider.in/india/news/these-are-the-companies-manufacturing-covid-19-remdesivir-medicine-in-india/articleshow/76747405.cms

27. https://www.bbc.com/news/health-52036948

28. https://www.mayoclinic.org/tests-procedures/convalescent-plasma-therapy/about/pac-20486440

29. https://www.who.int/health-topics/vaccines-and-immunization#tab=tab_1

30. https://www.timesnownews.com/health/article/russia-may-approve-world-s-first-covid-19-vaccine-for-public-use-by-mid-august-report/628747

31. https://theprint.in/world/two-asian-pharma-companies-hold-key-to-oxford-vaccine-china-woos-asean-other-covid-news/470289/

32. https://indianexpress.com/article/explained/coronavirus-vaccine-update-pfizer-biontech-moderna-clinical-trials-6528581/

33. https://www.mayoclinic.org/diseases-conditions/coronavirus/in-depth/herd-immunity-and-coronavirus/art-20486808

34. https://chopra.com/articles/keeping-your-chakras-balanced-during-covid-19

9 798672 225913